Acknowledgment

First and foremost, I would like to thank God, the Almighty, for blessing me with the ability to come as far as I have today. All praises and thanks are to Him.

I would also like to take this opportunity, to thank my parents, family and close friends, who believed in me and have supported me throughout the journey of writing my first book.

To
each one of you, who have
the courage to express their feelings,
and especially to those, who
strive to be better than yesterday

Inspiration

"The heart on its journey towards God is like that of a bird. Love is its head, and fear and hope are its two wings. When the head is healthy, then the two wings will fly well. When the head is cut off, the bird will die. When either of the two wings are damaged, the bird becomes vulnerable to every hunger and predator".

(Ibn Al- Qayyin).

Our hearts, just like a bird, are on a journey to God. Our love for God is the basis of our worship, and our fear and hope are like two wings that propel us along the straight path towards our final destination.

Each wing is necessary for balance and survival. Similarly, love for God along with the hope to meet Him, and the fear to not displease Him protects us from all kinds of vulnerabilities that exist in our world.

Introduction

For most of us, when we think of a rose, we think of its beauty. But have you ever considered what truly makes a rose so beautiful?

For me, a rose expresses hope, growth, strength, and new beginnings.

Similarly, when I think of birds, the first thing that comes to mind, is of them flying. But when I *actually* think about what a bird represents, I think of freedom, power and courage. I admire the way they uplift their wings, and assertively soar into the sky.

Just like a rose, a bird is also inspirational. They each have a purpose, and they are both proof that miracles exist. I hope that my words inspire you. I hope that every time you read my words, they make your heart bloom with hope and fill your soul with strength, just like at the sight of a rose or a bird.

On the contrary, just as a rose has its thorns, we too, in our ways, have thorns. The pain, loss, adversities, tests and trials that we are "afflicted" with, they are *our* thorns.

But here's the point I am trying to make. Our thorns are what make us who we are today. We would not be the same without our faults and our flaws. We wouldn't learn how to get back up, if we didn't fall down in the first place. If we didn't struggle, we wouldn't succeed.

How would you bloom like a rose with broken petals, or soar like a bird with damaged wings, if your heart was unable to feel hope, faith, and trust in your Maker?

It is true; our hearts are just like a bird on a journey to God. There will be bad days just like there will be good days. Some days our faith will be high and other days it will be low. However, the thorns of a rose cannot stop the rose from blossoming, and our hardships cannot stop our souls from prospering or flying. I hope you find the courage to always bloom like a rose, and the freedom to forever fly like a bird.

To all of my readers across the globe, I give you...

A Flying Rose

Part I:

Sailing
Through The Storm

Intention is everything

I have learnt that life is a test
and so are the people in it

My father once told me,
"Be with the truth,
and be truthful with others.
For there is no competition
between what is true,
and what is not".

Sometimes God sends you people that He knows *are* good for your soul.
Other times, He will send you people that He knows *will* be good for your soul.

Maybe they were
put in your life,
so that you would
learn how to
put God first

A *good* heart with *good* intentions
will get you through the worst of times

There are some people who will come into your life and the reason behind that is very special. They were sent to help you become closer to God. How comforting is it to know, that God chose that particular person to help you grow, and to fill you with hope. God chose that specific human to bring you closer to Him. It's like God loves you, and loves that person *for* you.

There are very few people who
will *genuinely* want good for you.
Watch what they do, and
not just what they say

Let me tell you something.

When you wish bad for someone, when you don't want them to have something nice. Or when you don't want them to have "better" than you, it *will* backfire on *you*. Not them. Have you ever wondered why we are taught to want for others what we want for ourselves? Because that is where the blessings are. It's called being genuine, having a good heart and clean intentions. That's what it's about. Intention. So if you have bad intentions for someone else, for no real reason whatsoever, then you're only setting yourself up for a big fall. God is always with the good hearted ones. That's why I stand by, good intentions getting us through the worst of times.

Because even if we can't see what's coming,

He can.

A *friend* should be someone you can talk to openly about what's going on in your mind and heart, without feeling as though they would judge you.

If you don't know how to be
a good person, then nothing else
really matters

If words mean anything,
time will show you

Isn't it amazing how certain people come into your life?
Isn't it incredible how God works in mysterious ways,
causing certain people to cross paths with you?
It is true, how everything happens for a reason and how
there's a purpose with so much meaning behind it.

And you know how it's only natural for us to sometimes
wish that we could read other people's minds?
Well, the more I think about it, it's *not* about reading other
people's minds.

It's about understanding God's beautiful and *loving* signs.

The evil eye is real
but so is God.

You are
your *own* person
and that is
your power

A clean heart will
open beautiful doors

consistent love and
consistent friendship,
is what makes it all feel
a little more real,
and a lot less fake.

Love *isn't* addiction and addiction *isn't* love.

A love that can lead you
to paradise,
is a love worth seeking

Have you ever come to know someone who isn't like anybody
else you've met? They uplift you when you feel like you're falling
apart, and they make you smile at the most random times.
I mean, they don't even have to say much, or *do* anything.
They're just simply in your life, and are a huge part of you,
and you know in your heart that whatever happens,
they can *never* be replaced.

I've reached a point in my life, where even if I had only *one true* friend, it would be enough.

Because the truth is, not everyone who you think is close to you, wishes well for you. It's unfortunate and it's sad, but it's the way it is. There is a reason why jealousy is a disease; it destroys good deeds like fire burns wood. It's really not worth it. So I pray that God shows us who is true, and who is not. Those who are not, I pray He keeps them as far away as possible.

At the end of the day, if having a malicious mentality is what makes you happy, then by all means go ahead, ruin your own life. But at least have the decency, to leave those who *think* of you as a true friend, in peace. Because chances are, that once they are shown the truth, they're not going to want anything to do with you.

At all.

"and they will underestimate you.
So *let* them".

Be real
it's not worth
being fake

Maybe if we all
stopped trying
to make this world
a paradise,
maybe then, we would
all be much happier
deep within

Be honest.
You owe your heart
that much

Our problem is that we don't love ourselves, or we just don't know *how* to love ourselves. This is when we become sad and it builds up inside us, to the point where we don't think we are good enough. We don't believe in ourselves. But we must learn to love ourselves to be happy on the inside. We must understand that God made us all differently and we are all unique for a reason. We want love, and we want to *be* loved. But *how* can we expect to give love and be loved, if we don't love ourselves? Happiness is with God and God should be in our hearts. That's when we will *really* feel it.

That is when happiness will *truly* mean something

You can struggle,
but you can *still* succeed.

If you depend on God
you're already
winning

She was the bird
that never stopped flying

Even good people do bad things.
Nobody is perfect.
We are not designed to be perfect.
We are meant to have flaws.
We are always going to make mistakes.
Your sin is between you and God.
It's about realising that you've messed up.
It's about turning to God and seeking His forgiveness.
It's about learning and it's about *trying* to be better.

Your smile is precious.
Pass it on because the
world surely needs it

Everyone's success comes in different ways. No one is the same. You might see people succeeding with money. They may have their own business, a career or a family. On the other hand, some may not have as much. But that doesn't mean that they are not successful, or that they're not succeeding. They may not have a great job, they may not be *able* to have children, and they may not be as skilful or as talented as others.

But what if, they are those who struggle everyday trying to better themselves? What if they are those who use their time to constantly remember God?

What if they are those who yearn for their hearts to be connected to their creator?

Now tell me, isn't *that* what TRUE success is?

Putting yourself first
doesn't make you a bad person.
You are important as well,
and don't you forget it.

At times, the best thing one can do is to stay quiet.
There is so much to say. There's a lot going on in your
mind. Your heart feels heavy. You feel confused.
But sometimes, it's better to remain silent.
Take some time for yourself and breathe.
Don't let the chaos of this world disturb your inner
peace. Because nothing lasts forever, except your good
and bad deeds.
Sometimes, when you've said all that you can, it's
better to just stop, and let the answers come to you

Just because it's not happening right now,
doesn't mean it never will.

Something as little as saying "*Please God help me*",
can change your life in ways you wouldn't even expect.
I feel like, it's all about using the heart God blessed you
with, and being sincere with it.

"It's not about wishing for me,
it's about hoping.

I am a *hopeful* thinker".

Have you ever known anyone, who you clicked with straight away? The type of person, who you can talk to about anything and everything, without feeling uncomfortable?

You can share with them your most random thoughts, your fears, and sometimes even your deepest secrets. You feel like they understand you, especially when they are a million miles away. You have a strong connection between you, and every time you talk, that is your bond growing stronger.

You wish they were near so that you could just hug them, because they give you a feeling. A feeling on the inside, where your heart is smiling every time their name is mentioned, and your soul feels at peace, each time you pray for them. Have you ever felt that they are a part of you, in a way which you cannot really define? They are those, who are a million miles away, but still, reside right in your heart.

It was peace that he longed for,
nothing less and nothing more.
But there was only one place he
could find something so *pure*.
So I told him, have some faith
and don't stop knocking on
that special door

She's reserved but wild;
sensible but feisty
shy but knows her own mind
loyal and one of a kind
she's a keeper, but rare to find

Distance doesn't have to feel
empty if the heart is present.
Because no matter how far apart
you are from one another,
if your hearts are connected,
the absence between you will
only make you stronger

Soon you will see that eventually
everything starts to fall into place.
From your hardships to your happiness,
it is all on its way to working out perfectly.
Even if you don't know it yet.
Hold your head up high, do your best, and pray.
Remember, after every hardship, there is ease.
Good things are on their way

I hope the light in your heart grows,
to the point, where there is no longer
any room for darkness.

I know it can be hard, but it's much better
to be grateful for everything. Especially for the
things that seem to be going 'wrong' in your life.
Because things could be much worse.
Thank God they aren't.

...and then I realised, everyone is tested with what they love most. So whatever it is, don't let it come between you and God.

It comes down to priorities and prayer, and I pray that God makes you and I stronger. I pray He gives us the ability to encourage and inspire one another. May He guide us to the straight path, and help us grow into the best version of ourselves.

She was heartbroken,
yet she still believed.

beautiful things take
time. When you plant a seed,
it won't grow into a sunflower
over night. But when it's ready,
to bloom, you will realise it was
worth the wait

When she prayed,
she prayed from her
heart

Just because people don't share their problems doesn't mean they don't have any. Everybody has their own fair share of hardships. Everyone is tested in a number of ways, and everybody is different. Hence, even something as little as a smile could have a huge impact on someone else's day. You just never know.

A little bit of kindness goes a long way. After all, we are all going through the same journey, but in our own separate ways.

She's just a good hearted girl
with a few bad habits.

The moon,
The stars,
The sun
and the rain.
They all have a connection with the sky.
They all carry soul, they all symbolise hope
and they all give light. It's no wonder
I've always had this urge, to travel up
somewhere high, and just fly.

Respect yourself enough
to know your worth

and that's what made
her beautiful. Even on
her worst days, she
believed something better
was coming.

You don't need to have a lot of friends to have *real* friends.
Quantity is meaningless when it comes to your friendship circle.
It's the quality of those friendships that matter.
How you treat each other, how much effort each of you put in,
and how much love you show to one another.
That's what will count in the end.

I like boxing and baking.
I mean there's nothing like
a good cupcake and a badass
workout to remind you that
life is worth it.

She will make you
feel better
even when she's
feeling sad herself

Even a rose
can fly
the petals
are
proof

Faith makes all things possible;
and love makes them easy

-Two words

I believe the people we love,
we have loved once before.

and then she heard the raindrops
falling from the midnight sky.
So she raised her hands up high,
to the only one who always
hears her heart cry.

It's important to share a *real* friendship
with the person you love.
Because the best relationships are based
on friendship. If you find a friend in your
significant other, I feel like the relationship
is more likely to be successful.
Because *real* friendship lasts a lifetime, and
true love is friendship

Pray for what you want,
and pray for it hard

Don't let jealous people
destroy your happiness.
They envy you for a reason,
but that doesn't mean it's
your problem.

If love is blind,
it *can't* be *love*

She's not broken,
she is *healing*

She was the girl who loved to love. The type of girl who wore her heart on her sleeve, and when she loved, she would love wholeheartedly. She would put her ALL into that love. Her heart, her mind and her soul would all dive deep into that love. Not because she was senseless or naïve, but because she was gentle, kind and real. Magically real. They said she was the girl who would always get hurt because of the way she loved. But if it wasn't for that raw, honest and pure love, what would be the point of love?

Sometimes when you think of a place,
you think of a person.
It's like; you can be amidst a war,
and still experience something special.
It's never about the place; it's always about
that one person

Be the friend
you wish you
had

You are stronger than you know.
Never let anyone tell you otherwise,
because they don't know you, the way you
know yourself.
You've had your fair share of ups and downs,
you've been through tough times, and you've
come out much stronger on the other side.
You have God, you have family, and you have
at least one person that you can trust.
You have it made.

It was something about the moon
that made me want to live up there
with all the stars around me.
I'd be wrapped in light, even when
touched by darkness

Once she finds it in
her heart to love you,
she won't ever stop

"He challenged me
and *I do* love a challenge".

Sometimes your love for someone is greater than how much they get on your damn nerves, or how much they have hurt you in the past. It's like no matter what they do or say, somehow you always get through it. You can't ever stop caring for that person, and even if you so much as try, you won't stop caring. Because deep down you know that person, as a good, decent person. You know that beneath the surface, they have a *good* heart. You could get mad at each other, you could say things to one another in the heat of the moment, but at the end of the day *they* make you happy. Even through the worst of times they make you smile like no one else, and you know you could never find it in your heart to ever hate that person.

They were both as stubborn
as each other.
One wouldn't give up, and
the other wouldn't give in.
Little did they know, that
all they ever really wanted
for each other,
was happiness.

Don't give up on the one you love.
Maybe that's just what they need...
Love.

There are days where I just want to sit on a rooftop, under the moonlight, sip on hot coffee, and watch the stars shine bright.

Damn, that would make the perfect night".

Beneath all of his scars
and his hidden wounds,
There was a heart...

She's the kind of person
who loves to be happy,
but loves it more when
you are happy

I dare you to dance in the rain.
Take a walk in the rain,
stand still in the rain.
I dare you to embrace the rain.
It's soothing, it heals and it's a
magical waterfall from the
heavenly skies.

Love with sincerity in your heart.
Love with pure intentions.
Love with honesty.
This kind of love is rare
and irreplaceable.
This kind of love is beautiful.
Because it is this kind of love that is
real, and so damn worth it.

There is hope for everyone who thinks there is not.
Because as long as your intentions are genuine, and
you are consistently in touch with your creator,
nothing except good will come your way.
Be patient. The struggle may be bitter, but
the end result is always sweeter.

They say you can't have
everything you want,
but you can *surely* pray for it

There is no better gift than being in someone's Du'a (prayer).
The way I see it, is *that* someone is reaching out to the Lord of
the entire universe including the heavens, only to speak about *me*.
Now I'm not sure about you, but I truly believe that is a gift,
one that is priceless.
Nothing is more consoling than being in someone's heart when
they are praying to the Healer of hearts.

If you've got your mother's prayers,
you have got everything, and more

Maybe you're well on your way to getting exactly what you've been asking for, and everything that you want. But *maybe* your test is based on patience, faith and trust. So *maybe*, you should really think about that, before complaining and acting as though you don't have anything.

When *really*, you have been blessed with everything and more.

-To myself before anyone

You don't have to chase *real* friends.
They are those who will meet you halfway

If something is meant for YOU,
it is going to come to YOU.
It may take a few detours,
it might even get stuck in traffic.
But if it's written by Allah for you,
then no matter how long it takes,
it will get there, for *you.*

These days it's rare to find a man who cares about your thoughts, emotions and fears. It's rare to come across a man who genuinely cares about your wellbeing. It's not easy to find a man who would feel down, only because *his* woman is feeling sad, a man who doesn't judge you by your mistakes, doesn't care about your flaws, or who would pray for you when you need it the most.

But if you're ever blessed with a man like that, who is honest, loyal and selfless, thank God from your heart. Never take that man for granted, and never give up on him.

He is a gift from God, and gifts like him only come once in a lifetime.

Sometimes I wish
I was a bird.
All I would do is
fearlessly fly, and escape
somewhere far,
deep into the blue sky

Her heart is pure
and that is
her protection

Money won't buy you
happiness because true
happiness is priceless

A good heart will pray for you
even when you hurt it the most

He was the moonlight
on my darkest nights

It is rain
that grows roses;
not the storm

It doesn't matter how far you drift apart.
Some bonds were just never *meant* to break…

She was praying for him
and he was praying for her happiness.
So in essence, they were both praying
for the same thing. They were both
praying for each other

I think when you love someone, they will be
in your prayers no matter what.
Because they are in your heart and
God put them in your heart.
So when you are talking to the one who
 made your heart, about the one who is in your heart,
 how can it not be coming from a place of *love*...

Sometimes two people can be so different, but it's *those* differences that make them work so well together. It is those differences that help them grow as individuals and as soul mates. It's the differences that allow them to learn from each other and better themselves. Just because two people are "different", doesn't mean to say they are not compatible. In reality, it could mean they're perfectly meant for each other.

That's the thing about those two,
there was magic between their hearts.
Even if they couldn't be together in this life,
they would always value the memories they shared,
and no one could take that away from them

If someone is praying for you to be guided,
they're praying for God to protect you,
to help you, to have mercy on you, and to bless you.
They are praying for God to save you.
They are praying because they *love* you.

If it's written by Allah,
you'll find your way back
to each other, and not a soul
can stop it from happening

You can't hide
from what's inside
your heart

If you want to see a thousand miracles,
and witness signs of God, look deep into nature.
Watch the sunset, stare at the moon,
feel the rain on your skin, and sleep under the starlight.
If you want to understand everything better,
look deep into nature.
But use your heart, and not just your eyes

She's the kind of girl who
dreams of flying in the rain
and landing on a rainbow.

The rain is my shelter
for it is mercy from
the sky

"When you have the key
  to someone's heart,
  you have the power to love it
  So *love* it".

You can't admire a rose,
but ignore its thorns.

She chases sunsets,
not men.

Pray for miracles
because they exist
and they are happening
every single day

Even your tears
are a blessing

"You won't find *her* in any other woman.
The more you search and the harder you try
will only make you realise what you lost.
You were too busy playing with glitter,
when all along,
she was the diamond".

They may have stopped
talking to each other,
but they never stopped talking
to God about one another

Maybe you weren't meant
to get it, without praying
for it first

Together, they were
the perfect storm.

He gave her the stars
so she gave him her heart

They were so different
yet worked so well together

She was his angel
and he fought away her demons.
Together, they were
a match made in heaven

Your prayers are powerful.
They can take you to an abode
of radiant joy, that no eyes
have ever seen, and no ears
have ever heard

She loved him.
So she told the one
who made him

He thought he could break her.
But little did he know,
he would *never* own that kind
of power

Oh darling, there is a
major difference
between love and lust.
Do *not* get it twisted.

She wasn't attached.
She was *in love*.

You need all the prayers
you can possibly get.
Because you never know
which of those
will be accepted

How intelligent is a tree.
It teaches us to stay grounded,
to stand tall, and to have patience.
Even if it means that sometimes,
you will fall.

She is feisty but friendly.
I call her a wildflower

There are still a lot of things I don't write about.
A lot of stories I don't tell. A lot of feelings I don't discuss.
It doesn't mean that I don't feel it.
It doesn't mean it's not there, somewhere.
Sometimes there's things you can't say, things you can't
talk about, but they are things you *do* and *can* feel.
Sometimes words aren't enough.
Yes, words can be powerful, for sure. But sometimes,
what you feel in your heart is another level.
The heart carries another story and sometimes,
the heart is simply a world of its own.

But my dear,
your heart
deserves to be loved.
By *you*

She's a once in a lifetime
kind of woman and if you let
her slip away, it will be
your loss, not hers

They asked me, "Why do you love the rain?"

There is more to rain than tiny droplets of water falling from the sky.
The smell is sweet, crisp and clean. The sound of heavy rain is soothing, especially at night. Hearing it bounce off the roof and hit the ground is peaceful. Watching it drip gently down my window, is somehow healing. Yes, the rain heals. The rain is like a waterfall from the heavens. It comes with blessings, and it is showered with mercy. Even if a single drop is caught in your hands, it's untainted, and fresh enough for you to drink. But you know what I love most about the rain? It's that the rainfall is a time when prayers are readily accepted. A time when you ask God for something from your heart, and its most likely accepted. See, there's so much more to rain than you realise, so much clarity. The rain is pure in every shape and form, and how can you *not* love something so pure?

You could have the best
intentions, and there would
still be some, who will think
the worst of you

Do not underestimate any good that you do.
Because God judges your hearts intention,
and the smallest act of kindness could be your
ticket to a home in heaven.

"Nothing is simple.
 But you have to think far
 to get there"

-From a special soul

Take care of your heart,
it is what will set you free

Imagine if heaven is planned for *you*.
Written for *you*. Meant for *you*..
and so, what if you struggling right now,
is just part of the plan. What if these
trials are preparing you for a much
better life. Where mountains are made
of musk, and your youth never fades away.
What if all of this is for the better?
For eternal happiness
For ultimate success
For Paradise...

Part II:

**From My
Heart
To Yours**

Special people don't get replaced

A true friend is someone
who prays for your happiness
because they want for you,
what they want for themselves.

Thank you for being my *true* friend

She's down to earth, carries a humble heart and exhibits a strong mind. She appreciates the difference between right and wrong, and no matter how hard it gets, she always keeps her intentions clean and pure. Sure, she's not perfect, no human soul is. But she's one of a kind, loyal, honest and rare to find. She craves to be close to her creator, in a way that even words can't define. She treasures her goal in life, so trust me, if you're ever blessed with a friend like her, you'll never be left behind

Distance and time never let you be mine.
But, there *is* God, and where there is God,
anything is possible.

You know how the stars are so far away?
All the way up in the sky, but they're *still* there…
and no matter what, they are *always* there.
Well it's a bit like my love for you.
You could be eight hours away let's say,
or you might be half way across the world.
But it doesn't matter because you are *still there.*
It's like loving you from afar, you know?
Just like a beautiful shining star.
That, is what *you* are

I told God I want to share
the happiness He gives me,
with you. I told Him
because He's the
only one who can make
it happen.

You know
what warms my soul?
Watching the sun paint skies
in beautiful hues,
and having deep conversations
with you, which make me
lose track of time

I think of you all the time.

There was a time when I planned to forget you, because at the time, it's what seemed easier. It's what seemed best. The truth is I don't know *how* to forget you. Because forgetting you would mean completely changing my heart and mind. It's weird because even though you're not in my life like you used to be, you're still in my heart. You are still in my heart, which means you were never really gone at all.

I have a friend in you,
a *real* friend, and that's
the best part

You were sent to me for a special reason.
Why else would Allah let me love you?

We are so far
yet so close

She is a beast in her own way. Fierce, crazy and smart.
To start the day she will plan, pray and slay.
Of course she has flaws, but that's what makes her perfect.
No matter how many setbacks she's been through,
she'll get herself back up, brush the dust off, and move
forward to the next day.
Because she has a strong heart, and a fire in her soul.
She's full of love, she is brave, resilient and she's relentless.
She can be a sarcastic queen but the most loyal person you will
come across.
She has her wild days, the same way she has her sad days.
But she's unstoppable and her smile can light up the darkest of
days.
She flies like a bird and blooms like a rose.
She can stand alone like a wolf and isn't afraid to roar like a lion.
She is magic.
She is a gift.
She is a woman.

I will fight for you
through the heart of my prayers,
and I have no intention to stop,
until the day you become mine

I don't want the world,
I just want *you*

Maybe we're not together now
because perfection doesn't exist
in this world.
It's designed for the next

I asked God
to *save* you for me.
Because that's all
I can do for now.

I pray for the day we are reunited
and our souls are reconnected, by the one
who loves us the most.
I pray He grants us the perfect union with
His mercy and His blessings.
I pray we can spend the rest of our lives with
each other, and grow to love everything about *Him*,
together.
I pray we are destined to meet again after this life.
where everything lasts, and nothing ends.

If we ever have to go
our separate ways,
promise me one thing.
Promise me that no matter what,
you will always keep
me safe,
locked inside your heart.

He merges the day into night, and the darkness into sunlight. Maybe that's how the distance between the U.S and the U.K, can connect and meet halfway. A little like our friendship, wouldn't you say?

So whenever you are feeling in need of His infinite mercy, look up high and search for the stars in the sky. Look up and remember, it is *He* who created the sunset and the sunrise.

The very same way, He did you and I.

I feel blessed
to know,
that the path from
your heart to mine,
was written before
our time

"Why would I be happy
    if you're sad?"

-From a part of me

You'll find me where the moon is.
Because the moon always
sheds light,
even on the darkest nights,
and just like the moon
I will always be here for you,
shedding light and
whispering prayers of hope
and happiness,
for you

May your heart
be joined with
the one you love

"I wanted you to have everything.
  I wanted you to be with somebody who
  could give you everything".

"But what is *everything*, if it's not with you?"

I hope Allah makes the one you love
become the *right* life partner for you.
May He grant you both to
reunite in paradise, where there
are gardens beneath which rivers flow,
that are whiter than milk and
sweeter than honey

"The connection I have with you,
  I want with no one else".

She always knows what to say.
When you're sad she will make you smile.
When you're happy she will smile with you.
She'll remind you of God through your worst times
and your best. You might not have been friends for long,
but I swear it will feel like you've known her since childhood.
Her confidence will inspire you, yes that's right.
She's sincere, strong and gentle. Oh so smart, and
far from judgemental. She's one of a kind, you know?
A true gem that is rare to find. Believe me,
she will light up your day even if the sky looks dull and grey.
Be it, heavy rain or the worst kind of snow, she will always be
The Perfect Rainbow.

He felt like
Home
to me

Maybe we were meant
to find ourselves; before we
found peace and tranquillity
with each other

We will meet again soon.
I don't know when or where.
But I'm sure God will let us
be together in the next life,
if we're just not meant, in
this temporary one.

The bond between
your heart and mine,
reminds me very much
of how the moon always
shines.

It shines on Earth, miles apart,
yet it *always*
envelops the Earth with light,
and the Earth never fails
to reflect back..

as if to respond...

"I am still here, just like you are"

May you never
stop hoping for the best,
from the *absolute* best

I love how God
wrote you into my story.
May He keep you there,
blessed and always happy

You're like a star.
Because even when
the darkness surrounds me,
you're the light that makes
my heart shine bright

I could never watch a sunset
without *you* on my mind

They told me
to listen
to my heart,
and all I heard,
was your name.

She is a thinker. A *deep* thinker.
When she talks you can feel her opening up.
Her heart opens, but only to a certain limit depending
on *who*, and *what* you are to her.
She loves sipping on her coffee, and her herbal teas.
She enjoys reading and taking photos of everything beautiful –
including cherry blossom trees.
There is something deep in her eyes, and if you look carefully,
you will see an inspirational soul, who is not afraid
to be different.

Promise me
you will always
remember me in
your prayers,
especially when I'm
gone

I believe that if you
are meant for me,
God will bring you
back to me.

"But *where* am I supposed
to find another *you* from?"

There is something *beautiful* amongst us.
Something strong, and something raw.
A bond that is unbreakable, a connection
that is effortless.
Although there is distance, our eyes witness
the same moon and the same stars.
It's a little like the sunset.
A stunning horizon in the far, wrapped in
soothing sunlight…
The sunset between us

You told me to travel,
to go and do what I've
always wanted to do.
You said, "Go and visit
the moon and see the stars".

But what is the point?

What's the point in seeing the moon and
the stars, if it's not with you?

You understand my heart
as if it is your own.
Now you know why I call you
my soul sister

I pray you are written for me
and I am written for you.
I pray we are the *best* part of
each other's destiny.

Sometimes I think
of all the pain I caused you,
and all I want to do is take it back

You took my
heart
to a place,
where no one else
could

A sky full of stars,
yet she still chose him
over and over again

Honestly, I never
knew *love*,
until I poured my
heart out to Allah
about you

"Let me be clear, if my love
for you was 'mistaken' for lust,
you would *not* be in my prayers.
Because I don't talk to God about
waste, I only talk to God
about what matters and what is
real"

You may not be my blood,
but you will always be my
sister

When I look at the moon
I think of you.
My heart feels at peace
because I know that
you see it too.

Your mamma deserves
a medal and more.
She raised my hearts best friend

What if, you and I
were *meant* to part ways,
only so that we could find
each other again

One day, I hope
you find it within
yourself,
to turn to God
and realise,
it is *Him* who
you need the most.

Her walls were up high,
and only *you* were able
to tear them down

Don't doubt your prayers.
You're talking to the one
who really can make all
of your dreams come true

May God turn your
heart back to me, and
break every obstacle that
is holding us back, from
truly being with each other

She deserves the best
She deserves light in her eyes,
sweetness in her smile,
and peace in her soul.
She deserves a real man.
One that will wipe away her tears
for every time she's sad.
A man who will comfort her
with the warmth of his heart,
and a man who will give her strength,
every time she falls apart.
She's one in a million
and she deserves love.
Not the everyday type,
rather the *purest* form of love.

I still pray for you,
I just wish you knew
how much

I hope we meet in Paradise,
Because over there nothing will ever die,
and every soul will get what
they truly desire

If there's one thing I know about us,
it's that there is no chance we met for no reason.
Because two souls with a connection like ours,
do not meet by coincidence or by accident.
This unique bond we share was written beautifully
before our time, and this friendship was meant for a
lifetime

Stay loyal, it suits you

-Advice from SA

I'm sure
my heart was *meant*
to ask for yours

She overthinks
She does it frequently
She's kind too, always speaks from her heart
More so, when it's something she's passionate about.
She doesn't give up easily, but worries more than she should
She wants to be understood because it hurts being misunderstood.
Particularly by those who are very dear to her
She's a special star. Always in search for light, from
the one who makes the moon shine at night.
She's soft but smart. So she knows,
that even if they try to destroy her happiness,
they will *never* tear her apart

I pray for you because
I know only *He* can keep you safe

I feel like our souls
have met before.
In some other place,
at some other time,
and our hearts have
been friends since then

With a heart like yours,
may you be destined for
greatness

I hope we find each other again,
and I hope we're in a much
better place than before.

Our connection is such,
that even if we lost our
way for a short while,
it would *still* be there

I could never hate you. Ever.
You came into my life with the will of Allah.
For a specific reason, we were meant to cross paths.
We were meant to learn from each other.
The good *and* the bad. Even though we've gone our
separate ways now, I admit, there are times when it hurts.
But at the same time, when thoughts of you crowd my mind,
I can't help but smile. And it is then that I realise,
you may no longer be in my life, but there will always
be a home for you in my heart.

I can't wait for the day you realise your worth to me.
You will be the happiest, and that's all I want to see

He took care
of my heart,
with his

You.

When I think about *you*, I think about how much you have changed my life just by being in it. Every time you cross my mind I instantly smile. Sometimes I feel like you have to be the most interesting person I know, and in more ways than one. You have one of the kindest hearts. When I feel sad you never fail to uplift me, you always make me laugh, and I feel safe inside, knowing I've been blessed to know a soul like yours. You always comfort me with your words of wisdom, and you're so humble that most of the time you don't even realise the affect you have on me. You don't realise just how happy you make me. One day, I truly hope for you to finally understand this. I hope you know what you mean to me because you are a huge part of who I am today. I am more hopeful and I have faith in God like never before, and that is mainly because of you. I must admit, it took me a while to fully understand why you were so special, and I used to wonder why you are in my heart like nobody else. And now I know. You brought me closer to what matters, and God put you in my heart because that's where you were meant to be, from the very start.

For you I pray,
May your heart
always be connected
to the one who
made it

Part III:

**Surviving
The Storm**

He has 99 names,
and if you read carefully,
every single one of them
spells love and hope

Trust the one whose promise is true

There is nothing in the heavens and the earth which is not controlled by God. Not even a leaf falls, but that He knows about it. So every time you make Du'a, each time you speak to God, remember this. Remember you are talking to the only one who can help you through your difficulties. The only one who has power over the entire universe, and the only one who knows what is inside your heart.

Because He's the one who made it.

We're all a little broken,
but we all have Allah too.

Anything is possible for Allah.
He only has to say "BE" to it, and it *will* BE.
So my advice to you would be, don't lose hope.
Don't get lazy when you ask your Creator for
what you want.
Ask Him with a full heart and don't stop asking Him.
Because He hears everything, *even* the whispers
of your heart. He knows what you want,
what you deeply desire and what will make you happy.
But only *He* can give it to you,
so **never** stop asking.

It doesn't matter how many days go past.
It doesn't matter how long it takes.
He knows what is in every heart and He is aware
of your intentions.
He can hear your thoughts as well as your voice.
Call out to Him day and night, because He will
always answer, and He will never let you down

Sometimes, certain things are not meant for you in this life. There are always reasons behind that, but you and I don't have the wisdom to see what's behind the wall in front of us. Allah does though. He knows what to give you and when to give it to you, and no matter what, He will always do what is best for you. Even if you may not understand it, one day you will.

You will.

He knows that your heart
is hurting,
and He knows how to fix it.
As He is Al-Jabbar.
The one who can
fix anything that is broken.

Always hope for good things.

Because Allah says, "I am as my servant thinks of me".

Meaning, Allah is able to do whatever we (His servants) expect Him to do. So from this I've learnt, that hoping and expecting the best from Allah is really important. Especially if we want to remain positive, even throughout the most difficult times.

If we want Allah to relieve us from our hardships, open the doors of mercy for us, and to grant us ease and guidance in our affairs, we *have* to have hope.

We *have* to believe *only He* can save us through our storms.

We *have* to have conviction in our hearts when we call out to Allah.

Because *that* is hope. That is hope in Allah.

And hope in Allah will always lead to peace and happiness. Without doubt.

If you're sad or you're having a bad day,
please remember this…
Allah can change the state of hearts.
Because Allah is the turner of hearts
and your heart, and my heart,
is in Allah's hands.

Allah tells us in the Q'uran,
"Call upon me, I will respond to you" (40:60).
So what makes you think He's not listening to you?
He heard you before the words even came out
of your mouth. That is the beauty of Allah,
we don't even have to say anything
and He already knows.

There's always a reason for why things happen the way they do. We don't always see it. We don't always know.

But God *does*.

He sees all that we don't. He knows everything that we don't have the wisdom to understand. That's why we are better off depending on Him, and relying on Him only. Through all the good and all the bad.

Because the truth is, there is no one who can protect us like Allah, and there is no one who knows *how* to heal us, but Allah.

He gives and gives and gives.
Even when we don't ask.
He is Al-Wahab
The Giver of all

"and even if only Allah
knows of the good in your heart,
remember that is all you need,
and all you will ever need".

God has a plan for each and every one of us.
He doesn't make mistakes.
It all comes down to your faith and your trust in Him.
Do you *believe* He can suffice you?
Do you *trust* He is the only one who can truly save you?
Because He is.
He's the *only* one who has power to make all impossibilities,
possible.
Remember, it's never too hard for God to make your
dreams come true.

He plans to bring you closer to Him.
Because in the end that is all that is
going to matter.

No one
is your friend like
God

Make the right intention,
and then watch how He
opens miraculous doors
for you. Because He is
Al- Fattah –
He who opens *all* things

It doesn't matter if you have the whole world on your side, or if you have no one. As long as you have Allah you don't need anyone else. That's why it is better to keep talking to Him and to keep in touch with Him. Whether it be on your way to work, driving to the grocery store, or when you're cooking at home. It doesn't matter when or where. Nor does it matter whether it's something small or big.

Allah has promised us that if we take one step towards Him, He will come running to us, and we all know, Allah does *not* break promises.

Sometimes when you want something really bad,
you don't always get it in this life.
You get separated from it.
But your prayers, your effort and your time,
none of it goes to waste.
None of it is forgotten by Allah.
He knows what your heart wants, and maybe He's
not giving it to you in this life, because He's saving it
for you to have, to hold, and to *keep* in the next life

Sometimes in life you have to make hard sacrifices.
It'll hurt and of course you will feel sad, but the strength
that you use to make that sacrifice, is *not* forgotten by Allah.
He won't let you suffer without allowing you to succeed.
He won't let you feel pain without giving you relief.
He won't forget the effort you put in, the prayers you made
at night whilst crying your heart out, or the time you spent
having good intentions. Allah loves you 70 times more than your
own mother. 70 times more than your own mother!
He might not give you what you truly want in this life,
but He will give you everything and more in the next life.
Everything, and more.

No one can hurt you
when you are under
Allah's protection

It's true.

We should never let anyone have such control over us,

where *they* are the reason for *our* happiness and *our* sadness.

Because only Allah has that level of power.

Happiness and sadness comes from Allah, good times and

bad times come from Allah. Everything we seek,

everything we want, is with Allah. People won't always be there.

But Allah will, and Allah is. He is near, and he is closer to us than

our jugular vein. So when you feel alone or upset, or even when

you are the happiest you've ever been, turn to Allah first.

Lean on your creator before you lean on His creation

If you're looking for love,
but you're not running towards
the one who *gives* love, and owns *true* love,
how do you know if the love you seek
is even real?

Ask God for help before
asking anybody else.
Because nobody has got your back
like the one who you belong to

Almost everything in life comes with some sort of price.
But if you think about it, life itself is about our relationship
with God. That's what I believe anyway, and *that* is priceless.
Talking to God about everything, including our worries,
struggles, deepest fears, our happiness and success.
It is all from Him. I feel like if we strive to be better than
yesterday, and if we make it a habit to build and maintain
a connection with God, I feel like our hearts would be more
at peace. In general, life would be better. Remember,
if you be mindful of Him, He will be mindful of you.

If two hearts are meant to be together,
if they are meant to be joined and filled with
love and mercy for one another, then *nothing*
anyone does can alter that.
It doesn't matter what they have been through.
It doesn't matter if it seems impossible right now.
It doesn't matter if you feel like there's no going back.
Because Allah is the owner of every souls heart.
Our hearts are in Allah's hands. He is the turner of *all* hearts.
He has the power to do *what* he wants, *when* he wants.
So if two hearts are meant to be, they *will* be.
No matter what

If you believe in God,
know that He will never burden you
with what your soul cannot cope with.
Know that no matter how hard people try
to make your life difficult, God won't let them
break you.
If you have hope and faith in your Maker,
He will always make a way out for you.
He will grant you the sweetest escape and
give you amazing things, from where you can't
even imagine

We all want a way out from suffering, a way out from the hurt and heartache.

Nobody enjoys being hurt or sad. And Allah tell us that whoever fears Allah, He will make a way out for them and provide them with what they need, from where they cannot even imagine. (The term "fear Allah" is about being God conscious and being willing to please Allah).

Another thing Allah tells us, is that whoever places their trust in Him, He will suffice them. Because He has already set a time for everything and He never burdens a soul with what they cannot deal with. He will *always* bring ease after every difficulty. This teaches me that no matter what, there will always be a way out.

Even when the entire world tells you there isn't.

If there is anything I have learnt about supplication, it's that the key is to be:
consistent,
sincere and
to have **conviction** in your heart.
They are the three components that truly add value to your prayers to God.

Even if things seem impossible right now,
I mean whatever your situation, problem or issue is right now,
don't rule God out, from any of it. Because God is who makes
miracles happen. God is able to bring peace to your heart.
God is who removes difficulties from your life, and God is
who blesses you with the happiness you deserve.
If God wills for something to happen, he says "BE",
and it will *be*.
You have a gift inside you. It is called D'ua (supplication).
Use what you have been gifted with to get closer to the only one,
who is able to grant you everything your heart desires.
Only God can give you what you *truly* want.
Whether it be a car, a house, a job, curing an illness, happiness,
to be with the one you love, peace or a home in heaven.
Nothing is worth giving up on if you have God.

Not a soul can separate
what God has joined

When I need to feel hope and when I want to feel hope,
I tell myself that Allah's mercy is greater than anything in
this world.
And to be honest, I always want to have hope in my heart.
I never want to lose hope.
Hope in Allah is what keeps me going.
It is what makes me believe.
Sometimes as humans, we find it hard to feel hopeful.
When life takes a left turn, it becomes easy for some of us
to lack hope. But when that happens, I have to remember that
no matter what is happening, it can NOT and will NOT
beat Allah's mercy. Nothing bad in this life can overtake
Allah's mercy.
That is the thing about Hope. Allah is the heart of hope,
and when hope is buried deep in our hearts,
we can *only* find Allah there.

You won't succeed without
the one who gave you life.
That's impossible

If you have the right intention
and your heart is full of sincerity,
and you're putting in the effort to do good,
do you *really* think that Allah will turn you away,
or turn away from you?
Allah loves you, and loves it when you call out to him.
Remember that.

Talking to God is never a waste of time.
In fact, there is nothing negative about pouring
your heart out to the one who made it.
When you develop a habit of telling Him anything
and everything at random times of the day,
you will notice that things change, in a good way.
Even if it's the smallest change, you will generally feel
better and free within. You will become extra hopeful
and stronger, both mentally and emotionally.
And eventually, you will come to realise that no one
will ever understand you the way He does.

He can change your situation
in all the ways you don't know how

If Allah can give you everything you have right now,
what makes you think He can't give you even more?
Sometimes life feels slow, and you find it hard to be
patient, you can't wait anymore because everyone
around you is getting everything they want.
But you see, maybe that's where *your* test lies.
To see how strong your faith is, knowing your Lord will
come through.
Just like He always has and He always will.
Remember, when the time is right for YOU, then
and only then will everything fall into place for YOU.
In fact, if you think about it, it is *already* starting to
fall into place...

Allah *knows* who you love.

He knows of all your secrets that are hidden in your heart.
I know it's easier said than done, but you don't have to
be scared. Of course, it's only natural to fear the unknown.
But I want to remind you that Allah is with you… and I pray
that whoever it is that your heart is holding on to, I pray Allah
makes them the perfect one for you

Where there is God,
there is pure light

None of us know what is going to happen tomorrow, or today. Or even in the next hour. But what's important is to understand that Allah is always there.

He's always listening to us even when we don't realise it. I think this is beautiful. It's beautiful to know that when we spend our time worrying and stressing over life, Allah is right there with us. He knows what is bothering our hearts. He knows we are struggling with peace of mind. He knows and He's right there. So, whenever you're worried about something, reach out to Him, and hold on to the rope of faith.

Because He is As-Salam - The Source of Peace.

And He is Al-Basit - The Reliever.

He hears everything I say, witnesses everything
that I see, and knows what I feel in my heart.
He knows what I want, he knows what I need.
He understands that I feel life can be unfair.
He knows everything and He's listening, He's there.
That's what gets me through.
Through all the tough times, the confusion, the pain.
Everything is just so much better because of Him.
It all means something true, something worth holding on to.
Because I know, that without Him, nothing would ever
make much sense, and I would never get better.
He is my creator. He is God, and He is what's real.

Even the strongest
person needs God

Have you ever wondered that maybe the reason why you
are constantly tested with hardships, is because God loves you?
Have you ever thought about why you are always having to
battle with your own soul? Sometimes it can feel like you are
cheating with your own heart right?
Because of the chaos around you, and now and then it comes to a
point where you are always tearing up.
But have you ever thought that maybe this is all happening to you
because this is God's way of bringing you closer to Him?
So that you may grow stronger as a person.
So that you can finally understand the true meaning of love, before
you value and appreciate anybody else, more than you should
Him

There is nothing that Allah can't change.
It is He who makes broken hearts beat again
Don't forget that

If Allah knows your heart is clean and that you have good intentions, do you really think He won't make your life easier for you? Do you really believe He won't shower his mercy upon you? Because let me tell you, He always will. Allah loves what is pure, good and clean. So, if we made it a priority to keep our hearts in the best condition, we wouldn't have much to worry about, would we?

-Just a thought.

When you want something, tell Allah.
Even when you don't want something in particular,
still, talk to Allah.
The point is everything you want, and don't want can
only be given and taken by Allah.
Your misfortunes, your blessings, your pain and your pleasures
can *only* be granted and removed by the will of Allah.
So when you need the confusion to disappear, and when you
need to understand the what's and the why's, scurry towards the
light.
Run to Allah, He will soothe your heart and He will
comfort your soul, in ways that no one else could even try.

I believe there is something special about the night time.
Sometimes I feel like the night is more pure than the day.
Because I feel like it is a time when we are deeply in touch with
our emotions, much more than we would be during the day.
But you know what really makes the night truly beautiful?
It's that Allah comes down to the lowest part of heaven, only to
see if any of us are in need of His mercy, His help and His
forgiveness. It's that last third part of the night, when Allah is
asking those of us who are awake, if we need or want *anything*,
that He may grant it to us.
So if you are suffering in any shape or form, and you feel like you
have no one to talk to, be sure to call out to Allah, especially at
night.
Pour your heart out because this is a very powerful and precious
time between you and Allah.

Tell him everything
for He is the master of
all miracles

You don't know whose prayer will be accepted
when people are praying for your happiness.
And it's amazing how the angels pray for those who pray for us.
So, if you think about it...
Praying is so beautiful and has so many benefits.
It's a win – win situation.
Because you can *never* lose when you pray.

There is nothing stopping you
from talking to God.
So pray for what your heart wants
and don't stop

You have to BELIEVE that God is capable
of giving you what you're asking from Him,
before you even ask Him

Don't worry if your life is hurting right now.
Because your heart is in the best hands-
In Allah's hands, and Allah can change the
condition of all hearts.
Anything is possible and anything can change.
You just have to be willing to run to Allah and
to take your whole heart with you

When you know in the midst of your heart that no matter what, God will come through for you, and He will rescue you from your fears, you won't let negative thoughts trap you.

You won't let those thoughts get the better of you and defeat you. Because you know, that despite all of life's tough challenges, there is a God. A God who sees everything, knows everything, and understands you better than you understand yourself.

So when you're feeling anxious or scared, go to that same God with every ounce of your shattered soul. Because even you know, your God has a way out for you, and He is ready to help you.

Never give up,
speak with your heart
and trust your Maker.

"Everybody sins.

Sometimes it's so easy to make mistakes.

But it's *easier* to seek forgiveness from God.

Even if our sins were to reach the sky,

God would still forgive us.

Because His mercy is greater than the sins we commit.

Everybody sins.

But the best sinners are those who repent".

People forget, but God doesn't

The closer you are to God,
the happier you will feel.

The second you feel alone,
remember He is closer to you
than your jugular vein

Oh Allah,
make what I ask for,
to be good and pure.
For you only accept
what is good and pure

Oh Allah,
please grant my heart
to be deeply sincere,
every time I make D'ua
to you

If God puts you through it
God will get you through it

-From an inspiration

Your heart and your soul needs God
Remember, you have *everything* if you have God

The more you trust Him
the more at peace you will be

Dear Allah,

It's not easy living in this world. Nobody's perfect but sometimes, it's hard to even try. It's so easy to fall into traps with temptations everywhere. It's so easy to make a mess of everything and it's so easy to get things wrong. I know this life is a test and it's always going to be full of trials and hardships. I realise that everyone struggles in one way or another, we all experience pain and heartache during some point of our lives. But I have come to understand that all of this happens with good reason. You know, what I do not. There is a valid purpose behind all of this and I know that as life goes on, I will begin to see everything unfold.

I get that it's about getting closer to you because you know what is best for us. So I ask you from every corner of my heart, as a part of my journey back to you, make me amongst those whose heart is free and protected from hypocrisy, arrogance, envy, greed and hate. Make me of those whose heart is humble, kind, loving and true. Make me better Allah. But most of all, please make me be amongst those who is most loved by *you*.

He heard your prayer.
Trust His Timing.

Thank you for your time
and
Thank you for being a part of my journey

Instagram: @sa.official__

Made in the USA
Las Vegas, NV
01 February 2021